How to Make & Keep Friends: Tips for Kids to Overcome 50 Common Social Challenges

www.HowToMakeAndKeepFriends.com

How to Make & Keep Friends: Tips for Kids to Overcome
50 Common Social Challenges

ISBN: 978-1456313463

EAN-13: 1456313460

www.HowToMakeAndKeepFriends.com

This book is dedicated to our children and our inspiration, Dan and Aaron Shea and Megan and Trent Briggs. They have shaped our lives and allowed us to explore ways to help others make and keep friends.

Contents

Section #3: Tips for How to Be a Good Friend

Introduction for Parents and Educators

Welcome to **How to Make and Keep Friends**! Many kids struggle with social nuances which can make it difficult for them to form lasting friendships. To help kids during those times, parents and kids often need quick social skills advice that is easily understood and even easier to do in the moment. Our tips have been successful for children with mild to moderate social challenges. While some of the children who have learned these techniques have a specific special needs diagnosis, many do not. Any child who struggles socially and needs a little extra support will benefit from these tips. While we both feel that it is important to view the "whole" picture when it comes to a child and understanding the reason or diagnosis behind these struggles, this book is aimed at the more immediate need many parents and educators ask of us - the "what" to do rather than the "why" it needs to be done.

This social skills guide is designed to provide top ten lists for 50 social situations that are inherently difficult for children with social struggles to manage. We encourage you to read the lists, pick what you like, ignore what doesn't work for you or your child and add your own ideas in the margins. It's all about giving kids the tools they need to recognize any individual barriers to friendship they may be experiencing and maneuver through the shades of gray that come with social interactions. Whether your child has difficulties with maintaining comfortable personal space, joining groups, conflict resolution or even the more simple challenges of using good manners, you'll discover a list of quickly-applied suggestions to try. Perhaps this book will encourage you to create a personalized list to use with your child. Either way, we wish you all the best as you coach your child to social success!

Nadine Briggs
Donna Shea
January 2011

Introduction for Kids

Welcome to our book, **How to Make and Keep Friends**! We wrote this book for kids because we understand that making and keeping friends can be really hard to do sometimes. We help lots of kids learn how to get better at making and keeping friends, and with this book, we can help you too. You can choose to read the whole book, or just read the parts that you think will help you with your friends. Ask an adult to read it with you so they can give you examples of how these tips can help in your life. We believe that all kids have a friend out there waiting for them, and it's just a matter of time before you find the friend for you.

Nadine Briggs
Donna Shea
January 2011

www.HowToMakeAndKeepFriends.com

Section #1:

Tips for Common

Social Situations

1

How to Greet Others and Enter a Room or Place

1. Remind yourself before you arrive somewhere that you will properly greet the people you see.

2. When you enter a place or a room, enter quietly without flinging or banging doors or running in a wild manner.

3. Move in and away from the door so that other people can enter if needed.

4. Stop and look directly at the person or people you are greeting.

5. If looking at the person is difficult for you, make sure your shoulders are turned fully toward the person.

6. Say hello to the person or people.

7. If someone says, "Hello, how are you today?" you should answer, "I'm fine, thanks, and how are you?"

8. Observe any other people that might already be in the room and notice what they are doing and how they are acting – try to do the same.

9. Ask permission before touching or using anything.

10. If a parent or another adult is dropping you off, make sure that you look at them and say "Goodbye" or "See you in a while."

"It is generally agreed that "hello" is an appropriate greeting because if you entered a room and said "goodbye," it could confuse a lot of people."

-- Dolph Sharp

2

How to Make New Friends at School

1. Try to make just one new friend and not several friends all at once.

2. Be friendly and say hello to others.

3. Practice conversation starters with family so you're ready to talk with friends.

4. Remember to listen when others are talking.

5. Show you're friendly with your facial expression – practice in a mirror.

6. Ask to sit with the new friend at lunch or on the school bus.

7. Ask what kinds of things he or she likes to do.

8. Remember that other kids also want to make new friends so they may be interested in having you as a friend too.

9. Show you're friendly by helping others.

10. Throw out a feeler for a get-together. You could ask a new friend, "Do you like to swim? Maybe you could come over and hang out at our pool sometime?"

"Friendship is born at that moment when one person says to another, "What! You too? I thought I was the only one."

-- C. S. Lewis

3

How to Join a Group

1. Take a few minutes and observe what the other people are doing.

2. If the group is sharing a toy or is doing an activity, try not to grab or take things in an effort to join in.

3. If the group is doing something that you would like to do too, slowly move closer to the group.

4. Barging into the middle of the group will only make people angry.

5. Don't assume that the other people are going to invite you to join (they may not be paying attention and may not notice that you want to play).

6. If they don't ask you to join, standing around and waiting without saying anything won't work.

7. Sometimes a yes or no question such as, "Can I play with you?" is not the best question – other people might say no and exclude you. Try a positive including statement such as, "I'd like to play with you."

8. If you are nervous because you don't know how to do what the group is doing or know the rules of the game, you can ask someone to show or teach you.

www.HowToMakeAndKeepFriends.com

9. If the group is all laughing about something and you are not sure what it is, you can say something like, "Hey guys, what's so funny?"

10. When you do enter the group, don't jump in and try to take over or change the rules. It works better to find out what everyone is already doing and do the same.

"The hardest part is to find what's in common, and it can be hard to talk to people because you get shy."

-- Matt C.

4

Personal Space

1. If others are leaning away from you, you may be too close.

2. If others are taking a step back from you, you may be too close.

3. Imagine a hula hoop around your waist and don't get any closer than that to others.

4. Use the length of your arm to tell if you are too close (you shouldn't be any closer than within one arm length).

5. If you are knocking things over, then you are too close to those things and need to step back.

6. If you're not sure if you're too close, take a step back just in case.

7. When showing someone your drawing, toy or any object, keep it at least an arm's length away from their eyes.

8. If you like to move around a lot, be sure to sit or stand where you have enough room to move without bumping into others.

www.HowToMakeAndKeepFriends.com

9. If someone is too close to you, ask for a little space (nicely). You could say, "Excuse me, could you move just a little the other way please?" Or you could say "I'd like a little more space please."

10. If someone bumps you, before you react think about whether it was on purpose or possibly an accidental bump.

"The essence of true friendship is to make allowance for another's little lapses."

-- David Storey

5

Eye Contact

1. Maintaining eye contact can be difficult for some people but it is an important social skill to practice.

2. Making eye contact with someone lets him or her know that you are listening and are focused on that person.

3. Some people see lack of eye contact as being rude and will think the wrong thing about you. They may think you're not interested, even if you are really listening.

4. If making eye contact is hard for you, start by keeping your shoulders turned toward the person to whom you are talking.

5. Try looking at their whole face instead of just their eyes to start.

6. Practice when you're alone by closing your eyes and imagining looking at someone else's eyes. Or, make eye contact with someone in a photo.

7. Eye contact can be tricky; you don't want to do it too little or too much. If you do it too much, people will think you are staring and may start to feel uncomfortable.

8. Practice with a friendly pet or a family member. Watch how they look away if you stare too long. Watch how they look at you and then look away.

9. Practice looking at someone's eyes (or your own in a mirror). Look away and then look back again as if you are talking to someone.

10. It's okay to be honest and mention to someone that you have trouble with eye contact, but you are still very interested in and listening to what they are saying.

"She tells the teens to watch their non-verbal cues: posture, eye contact, body language, dress. Attitude is everything, you are communicating every day – 24 hours a day."

-- Deborah King

6

Interpreting Body Language and Non-Verbal Communication

1. People use more than just words to communicate. In fact, 70% of communication between people is non-verbal (meaning messages sent with the body or face).

2. Practice looking at people and their body posture, gestures, and facial expressions to try to determine what they might be "saying" to you without words. Do they look happy or frustrated? Does the other person look interested in what you are saying or bored?

3. You can practice by making your own facial expressions in the mirror for different emotions. See if you can recognize them in other people. Have someone take your picture while practicing facial expressions.

4. Learn the non-verbal signs that people use. For example, someone looking at their watch frequently might be running late and may need to stop talking with you but isn't saying so with words. When you're running towards someone and they put their hands up, they are saying they don't want you to crash into them or hug them.

5. Watching your pet is a great way to practice since pets don't talk. Can you tell when your dog is happy, lonely or bored? Do you know when your cat needs your attention?

6. Pictures are another great way to learn – see if you can tell from a picture what someone is thinking or feeling.

7. Play charades.

8. See if you can guess what a person is thinking or feeling just by observing them.

9. Try to figure out if what the person is saying with their words or tone of voice matches what their body is telling you. Practice this with TV shows.

10. Parents and grown-ups can help practice this skill by asking "What is my body or face saying to you right now?" or "Can you tell by my voice and/or body what I am feeling or thinking?"

"The language of friendship is not words but meanings."

-- Henry David Thoreau

www.HowToMakeAndKeepFriends.com

7

What to Do if Someone Doesn't Understand Your Speech

1. It can be frustrating when you are trying to say something and people don't understand you, so try your best to not become angry.

2. When repeating yourself, slow down your rate of speaking and that may help the other person hear and understand you better.

3. Separate your words with a short silence between each word.

4. Try to talk a little louder since the person may not have heard you.

5. Look at the other person's face so they can see you are talking to them.

6. Try to pronounce each word's beginning and ending letter more clearly.

7. If you still aren't being understood, try another way of saying the same thing. For example, if you're not being understood when you say "I like playing dress up," you could try saying "I like wearing costumes."

www.HowToMakeAndKeepFriends.com

20

8. If after repeating yourself, the other person still can't understand what you're saying, try pointing if appropriate.

9. If they still don't understand you, look for someone else who may understand you and can help. Don't give up; what you have to say is important.

10. If this happens to you a lot, talk to your parents about getting some help to improve your speech.

"The best kind of friend is the one you could sit on a porch with, never saying a word, and walk away feeling like that was the best conversation you've had."

-- Author Unknown

Section #2:

Tips for Social Success

8

Staying on a Topic or

Changing Topics

1. Listen for key words to help you know what the topic is. For example, is someone talking about their pet, or how their weekend went, or the homework for today?

2. Keep your questions and comments on the same topic that the other person is talking about.

3. If the conversation becomes quiet, it's probably time to switch topics and ask the person a different question.

4. If you switch topics too quickly or without letting the other person know, they might not understand and they will be confused.

5. If you wish to change topics, use a topic-switching statement – for example, "this isn't on the subject, but I wanted to tell you…"

6. Try using a connecting statement so that the other person understands what your brain is thinking. For example: "I know that we were just talking about who had pets, and I wanted to mention that my aunt's puppy, Sam, had to go to the vet yesterday." If you just said, "Sam was sick," the

person would not know who Sam was or what happened.

7. Some people often get stuck on just talking about their favorite topic (weather, history, video games etc.). If this happens, say something like "I'm not really into _____," and then switch the topic.

8. Watch the other person to see if they might be looking bored with the topic. Maybe they are not paying attention anymore, or aren't looking at you, or seeming impatient.

9. Try making a list of other topics that you can talk about so that the conversation isn't always the same.

10. Even if a lot of topics aren't interesting to you, it would be helpful to know a little bit about different things that other kids talk about such as TV shows, popular songs, etc.

"Conversation should touch everything, but should concentrate itself on nothing."

-- Oscar Wilde

www.HowToMakeAndKeepFriends.com

9

Managing Conversation Challenges

1. When you don't know what to say in a conversation, a tip that always works is to ask the other person questions about themselves.

2. If you become nervous about talking to a new friend, practice conversation "ice breakers." They can be questions, such as "Have you seen any good movies?" Or "What's your favorite game?"

3. You can let the other person know you are listening by looking at them, repeating what they said in your own words or asking questions related to what they just said.

4. If you want to add your story to a conversation that is already going on, it's best to wait for a "pause" in the other person's talking and then tell your own story.

5. Remember to create pauses when you are talking so that other people can have a turn to talk.

6. If you are speaking to someone in a crowded room or at a crowded table, it usually works best to get closer to them rather than using a really loud voice or yelling across the table or the room.

7. If you think the other person might want to say something or is ready to change the subject, use a "topic changing" statement or a "finishing sentence" so that they know your story is over.

8. If you switch topics a lot and people seem confused, you can use a connecting statement such as "this is a little off the topic" or "that just made me think of..."

9. People who only talk about themselves are hard to talk to and often are not fun to be around. Remember to let the other person talk too and don't switch the conversation back to yourself or your own interests all the time.

10. If you tend to be a person that really likes one topic or gets stuck on your favorite interest, try to learn a little bit about all the popular things that the other kids are talking about at school so that you can join in conversations about different things.

"Lots of times you have to pretend to join a parade in which you're not really interested in order to get where you're going."

-- Christopher Morley

www.HowToMakeAndKeepFriends.com

10

Sharing Versus Bragging

1. Think about words that are used that can make the difference between sharing and bragging (avoid any "mine is better than yours" words).

2. Ask if the other person wants to see or hear about your new toy/game/experience.

3. Respect the person if they don't want you to share your toy/game/experience by not sharing it (even if you really want to).

4. Show/share without commenting on whether the other person has one.

5. Let them respond to it without you telling them how wonderful it is.

6. Offer to let them touch or use it.

7. Take turns with it.

8. If your friend seems jealous, put it away and don't discuss it anymore.

9. If you're accused of bragging but you didn't mean to, say "I didn't mean to brag, I just wanted to share." If you feel like someone is bragging to you,

you can say, "That feels a little bit like bragging to me."

10. Watch the other person's reaction to your sharing and end it when they start to look away or otherwise look bored.

"The true spirit of conversation consists in building on another man's observation, not overturning it."

-- Edward G. Bulwer-Lytton

11

How to Control (Modulate*)
Your Voice and Body

1. A venue is a place such as school, a sports arena, a library, etc. Think about the appropriate voice level you should have in each venue. For example, it's important to whisper in a library, but it's okay to cheer at a sports arena.

2. If you are unsure of the level of voice for a venue, you can observe other people and match your voice level to theirs.

3. Look at the person or people you are talking to. Do they look "uncomfortable?" or are they backing away? Can you tell if they are having a hard time hearing you? Try changing your voice, given the situation.

4. Pretend that your voice has a volume control button. Sometimes you might need to turn down the volume button up or down.

5. Look around at other people. Learn to ask yourself, "Is my voice too loud or just right for what is happening right now?" or "Is my voice blending in or sticking out?"

6. You can do the same if you are a quiet person. For people who are shy, it is important to practice using strength in your voice for other people to know what you are saying or to be able to stick up for yourself.

7. Do the same with your body. Notice if it is "too active" or "just right" for the venue or situation.

8. Some people have a hard time modulating singing or whistling or making noises – quite often, this can be annoying to those around you and you might not even know it. If someone asks you to stop doing any of these things, you should stop.

9. Our voices and bodies have a great deal of impact on other people, not just ourselves.

10. Think of a "signal" that good friends can give you if your voice or body is getting to a high level.

* See glossary for definition.

"To know when to go away and when to come closer is the key to any lasting relationship."

-- Domenico Cieri Estrada

www.HowToMakeAndKeepFriends.com

12

Public Versus Private Behavior

1. Understand that you have a private self and a public self – meaning that there are some things you can do when at home that you would never do in public.

2. When you are not in your own home (at a friend's house, movies, school, etc.) use the manners that your parents taught you.

3. Always say please and thank you.

4. Adjust personal undergarments in the rest room only.

5. Use a napkin while eating even if you think you don't need one.

6. No loud burping or other bodily noises.

7. If quietly burping, always say "excuse me" even if you think no one noticed.

8. Being really silly at home is fine, but be careful not to be too silly when in public.

9. When getting the attention of adult, use his or her full name by saying Mrs. or Mr. and then his or her last name.

10. Monitor yourself to be sure that your behavior doesn't cause someone to think bad or "weird thoughts" about you (see Weird Thoughts Tips).

> *"The art of living consists in knowing which impulses to obey and which must be made to obey."*
>
> -- Unknown

13

Weird Thoughts

1. When your private self is shown in public, people may get "weird thoughts" about you and you want to avoid creating weird thoughts in others.

2. Follow the rules in the Public versus Private Behavior section and think about if what you're doing will cause a weird thought or embarrassment.

3. Making funny faces in a reflection in public may cause a weird thought.

4. Talking to yourself or rolling around the floor may also cause people to be confused by what you are doing.

5. Being really excited when others around you are calm can bring unwanted attention.

6. If you're trying really hard to be funny but others aren't laughing, then you should stop.

7. Talking about a special interest when others aren't participating in the conversation (Star Wars, math, science, Pokémon, etc.) is a sign that you should stop.

8. Think about if your mom, dad or guardian were with you, would they ask you to stop what you're doing? If you think they would, then stop.

www.HowToMakeAndKeepFriends.com

9. Look at the expression on other people's faces to see if they are smiling nicely at you or giving you a look that isn't friendly.

10. If people are saying things to you like "what are you doing?" you are probably creating a weird thought.

"A true friend is one who thinks you are a good egg even if you are half-cracked."

-- Author Unknown

14

Things to Avoid So You

Don't Lose Friends

1. Don't repeat secrets that a friend tells you (unless it has to do with his or her safety – then tell an adult).

2. Avoid being or sounding bossy. Try saying, "how about we" instead of "you have to." For example, "How about we set up the train tracks in a circle" or "How about we play checkers first and then go outside?"

3. Allow your friend to have things their way and not your own way all the time.

4. If a friend asks you to stop doing something (even if you think it's funny) – adjust yourself to that feedback and - **STOP.**

5. Avoid doing things that might cause others to have "weird thoughts" about what you are doing (see Weird Thoughts Tips).

6. Don't blame others for problems.

7. Ask for things with your words – don't grab them with your hands.

8. Listen to your friend and talk about his or her interests – don't talk about just your interests.

9. Avoid teasing or annoying people to get them to pay attention to you.

10. Be a good sport (see Sportsmanship Tips).

"You can make more friends in two months by becoming really interested in other people, than you can in two years by trying to get other people interested in you."

-- Unknown

15

How to Handle Impulsivity

1. Being impulsive means doing or saying things without stopping to think first.

2. Try to think about the times when you tend to get the most impulsive (for example: during very competitive games/sports). Your parents can help you figure this out if you're not sure.

3. Prepare yourself for those times and think consciously that you may become impulsive so you can try to control it.

4. Try to freeze yourself when you feel like you want to do something that may not be well received by those around you.

5. Think about how you would feel if someone did the same thing to you (this takes a moment so you will have to freeze yourself to give yourself time to think).

6. If you do something impulsive and you are aware of it, admit it right away (for example: "Sorry, I shouldn't have done that.")

7. Don't get too down on yourself if you do something impulsive, just work on being aware of it before it happens.

8. Being impulsive can also be when you speak all your thoughts. Remember to keep some thoughts in your head, especially those thoughts with a lot of details.

9. Before those times when you tend to be most impulsive, prepare yourself with some high-energy physical activity. Run around outside, do jumping jacks, push-ups or other activities to spend some energy.

10. When you have strong feelings like excitement or anger, breathe slowly and deeply to calm yourself down, since these are times when you might be impulsive.

"Let the first impulse pass, wait for the second."

-- Baltasar Gracian

16

More Tips on Impulsivity and Interrupting

1. Some people have a "ready-fire-aim" brain (rather than "ready-aim-fire") that can make them forget to stop and think before they do or say something.

2. Interrupting others while they are talking is a form of impulsivity.

3. Touching other things or people without permission or grabbing are also other ways that people are impulsive.

4. Make sure that you ask permission with your mouth and not be impulsive with your hands. For example, "Is it okay if I touch your baby? She's so cute." or "May I borrow that magic marker after you are done with it?"

5. People sometimes interrupt because they don't want to forget their thought or what they want to say. Try to think about holding onto your thought in your brain until the other person is finished talking.

6. You may also stand near a person you need to talk to and wait for them to see you, which will signal to them that you need their attention.

7. Try to imagine a stop sign in your brain to help you stop and think before you do something impulsive that might get you in trouble. Or maybe even create a stop sign bracelet or charm to help you remember to stop and think.

8. If you tend to be impulsive when playing games – like grabbing cards away from people to read them or taking their turns for them – try to practice taking just your turn and then put your hands in your lap. Don't tell the other players what to do when it is their turn.

9. If you do something impulsive that causes another person to become upset or angry, it is important to take responsibility. If you didn't mean to do something, that's called an "oops" and you can say, "Oops, I didn't mean to knock over your tower. Let me help you fix it." If you do something "on purpose" that was meant to upset somebody, it's important to apologize and think of a way you could have handled the situation differently.

10. It's okay to "back-up and re-do" if you do something impulsive. For example, "I really didn't mean to knock over your tower. Let me help fix it. I'll try to be more careful."

17

How to Safely Handle Angry Feelings

1. Anger is a normal feeling, but there are rules for feeling angry. The rules are that it's not okay to hurt other people (with your body or words), to hurt yourself, or to damage property.

2. Talk to the person about how you feel. Use an "I" Statement such as "I feel angry when the rules of the game are changed because it doesn't seem fair, and I would like to play by the rules that are on the box."

3. Draw a picture of how angry you are and put it in the freezer to "chill out."

4. Pop or stomp your anger away with bubble wrap.

5. Use a strategy called "No Go Tell." You can say to the other person – "No, I want you to stop doing that." If that doesn't work, you can "Go" or move away from the other person to do something else. If the person doesn't stop or follows you, then "Tell" a grown-up that you have tried "No" and "Go" and need their help.

6. Go for a walk or ride your bike.

7. Rip up old newspapers or magazines that are in the recycling bin.

8. Dig a hole and put your angry thoughts in it. Then stomp the dirt over your angry thoughts.

9. Take a bunch of deep breaths and let the other person know that you are angry and need to walk away and take a break to calm down.

10. Ask yourself it the situation is really a "big deal" or a "little deal."

"When anger rises, think of the consequences."

-- Confucius

18

How to Handle Embarrassment

1. Try to remember that everyone has had really embarrassing moments (and lived through them!)

2. The best thing to do is to not make a big deal – if no one says anything, just be quiet and let it go.

3. You could say, "Gee, that was embarrassing!"

4. Laugh at your own mistake if you did something that makes you feel foolish. You could say, "I can't believe I just did that!"

5. If you accidentally say something embarrassing, you could say, "I didn't mean that how it sounded…let me try saying it again."

6. Try to remove yourself from the situation. Take a break, especially if you feel like you might cry.

7. Set an example for how others might react to the embarrassing moment, if you joke, they'll joke too and the embarrassing moment will pass quickly.

8. If the embarrassment was something that truly offended other people, a sincere apology is important.

9. If a friend is doing something embarrassing, you would be a good friend if you changed the subject, got them to do something else, or told them in private (in a nice way) if they don't realize that they are embarrassing themselves.

10. Remember that if you don't make a big deal of your awkward moment, people will forget about it.

"Only your real friends will tell you when your face is dirty."

-- Sicilian Proverb

19

Handling Strong Feelings
and Reactions

1. Remember that everyone has feelings and sometimes handling strong feelings can be difficult. It's harder to handle those strong feelings in public than at home.

2. Try to gauge your feeling to the situation. Are you reacting too strongly to something that is going on? Try to decide if it's really a big deal or a little deal.

3. Talk about your feelings by using "I" statements" such as "I feel _____ when _____, because _____ and I would like to _____. For example, "I feel really frustrated when someone isn't following the rules, because it isn't fair, and I would like to check the rules."

4. Try to understand what the other person might be feeling too. Offering an apology, shaking hands, or changing the subject might all help calm those feelings down.

5. Sometimes when you are having strong feelings of excitement, it's hard to calm down. Try to ask yourself, is my body and voice "too much" for this situation or "just right."

www.HowToMakeAndKeepFriends.com

46

6. If you are a person who worries, remind yourself that everyone worries, that no worry is "too weird," and that it is best to not worry alone. Sharing your worry with someone you trust always helps to make is better. It's the same for sad or lonely feelings. Don't keep it all inside.

7. Writing down why you're feeling strongly about something can help too.

8. Take responsibility for your feelings. No one actually can make you mad. You make yourself mad with your own thoughts about a situation.

9. Create a signal for you to use with adults who can help you manage those strong emotions if they happen a lot.

10. Remember that feelings are just feelings. Everyone has them and they are all okay. If very strong feelings cause problems for you a lot, it's okay to ask for help.

"In the end, who among us does not choose to be a little less right to be a little less lonely."

-- Robert Breault

20

When You Don't Understand

Or are Unsure of What to Do

1. Ask the person to repeat the question so you can hear it again. Even if you're feeling frustrated, try to use a friendly tone of voice.

2. Tell the person you need more time to answer by saying something like "Let me think about that for a minute."

3. Ask for clarification by repeating the question back in your own words to see if you understood it correctly.

4. "I don't know" is a perfectly acceptable answer if you truly don't know.

5. If you can't answer the question right away, tell the person that you need some time to think about it and will get back to them with your answer.

6. Ask their opinion about the question by saying, "I'm not sure, what do you think?"

7. Listen for key words in the question to clue you in, especially if the question is really long.

8. Look around the room. See if you can figure out what's going on by observing what everyone else is doing.

9. Ask them to draw it or act it out.

10. Ask an adult for help or ask another child that you are comfortable with to help you with the question or what you are supposed to do. It's okay to say that you are not sure.

"A mistake is to commit a misunderstanding."

-- Bob Dylan

21

What to Do When Others Aren't Listening

1. If you're talking to someone and they are looking away, consider the possibility that they can't hear you.

2. Try saying their name to get their attention and start talking again.

3. You could say, "I've got something to tell you" to get their attention.

4. Try using a slightly louder voice but be sure that it's not a yelling voice.

5. Think about how much detail you're telling your listener. If there is too much detail, the listener may stop listening.

6. Consider the topic you're discussing and if the listener is usually interested in hearing about that topic.

7. Is the person distracted by something else? Wait for a time when they aren't distracted to talk to them.

8. Is the person in a bad mood? Sometimes people

don't want to talk when they feel angry or are in a bad mood. It's best to wait until they are feeling better.

9. Are you telling them something because you think they want to hear it or because you like telling it?

10. Are you repeating something that you've already told them? If so, they may not want to hear it again even if you find it very interesting.

"Everyone has an invisible sign hanging from their neck saying, 'Make me feel important.'"

-- Mary Kay Ash

22

Assuming, Inferring, and Perceptions*

1. Accurately assuming, inferring and perceiving situations is very tricky as these are based on your own thoughts and ways of looking at things.

2. Inferring is looking for the hidden rules or messages. For example, you can infer that it is okay to take a piece of candy if there is a bowl left out on a table or that it is okay to take a book off the shelf and read it at a book store in one of their comfy chairs.

3. You can share your point of view or perception by using words like "in my opinion." That way you are sharing your own ideas and opinions but allowing other people to possibly have a difference of opinion.

4. There are as many assumptions; perceptions and inferences as there are individual people.

5. For some people, it is very hard for them to understand someone else's point of view. They only see things their way.

6. Sometimes perceptions and assumptions are not accurate. You may think that someone who isn't speaking to you is ignoring you, but maybe they are just very shy and don't know what to say. Or if you are sensitive to touch, you may have a perception that someone is trying to hurt you on purpose when they accidentally bumped into you.

7. Assuming, inferring or perceiving inaccurately can lead to difficulties in getting along with people.

8. If you find yourself having an argument over a difference of opinion or perception of something, sometimes an easy way to end the argument is to say, "well, maybe you're right" or "how about we just agree to disagree on this one?"

9. It is okay to ask a question to make sure that you are inferring or perceiving someone correctly. You could say, "I'm not sure you heard my question. Should I repeat it?" Or "I'm thinking that you just don't want to play this game. Maybe we can play something else?" Or, "Did you mean that to be funny? I didn't quite get it." In fact, the best way to overcome assumptions or misunderstandings is to simply ask a clarifying question.

10. Decide whether or not "facts over friendship" is worth it to you. Do you really want to have an argument or lose a friend over whether or not your opinion or knowledge of the facts is the absolute right one?

*See glossary for definitions.

Section #3:

Tips for How to Be a Good Friend

23

How to Decide Who Goes First
In a Game

1. Check the list of rules and see if it tells you who should go first – for example, the youngest player.

2. Spin the spinner or roll the dice and the highest number can go first.

3. Put pieces of paper in a cup with numbers on them to decide who goes first, second, third, etc.

4. Flip a coin. Ask your friend to choose "heads" or "tails." Flip the coin and if it lands with heads facing upward, then the person who chose heads goes first.

5. Play Rock-Paper-Scissors* and the best two out of three goes first.

6. Choose to be the "gracious" friend and tell the other person he/she can go first.

7. Have a grown-up think of a number from 1-10 and the closest person goes first.

8. The person with the closest birthday goes first.

9. Play the choosing games Eeny-Meeny* or Spuds Up.*

10. Remember that after it is decided who goes first, the rest of the turns (for most games) go in a circle to the left.

* See glossary for more explanation.

"You win some, you lose some. But you always try again."

-- Unknown

24

How to Share Fairly

1. Remember that common items or toys at an activity or in a classroom are for everyone to share, and do not belong to you or any one person. Saying "this is mine" is untrue.

2. "Hoarding*" toys or items to play with is not okay.

3. Offering to share before someone even asks you is a very good way to be a friend.

4. If you were playing with something and you put it down and walked away, it is now available for someone else to use it.

5. If there is only one item and many people that want to use it, you will need to take turns.

6. A good solution for turn taking is to decide how many minutes a turn will be and using a timer to time the turns.

7. See the Tips on "How to Decide Who Goes First" to see who gets the first turn.

8. If there is more than one item to share, such as trains, cars, etc., count up how many items you have. Then see how many people want to play and

each person gets the same amount (any extras can be put aside).

9. If there is more than one item to share, put them in a pile and let people take a turn choosing which one they want until they are all gone.

10. If you are sharing something such as a last piece of pizza or a piece of cake, let one person do the cutting and the other person choose which half they want first or offer your friend the biggest piece.

*See glossary for definition.

"The ones that give, get back in kind."

-- Unknown

25

Working Things Out

1. Lots of times you might hear adults tell you "go work it out" if you are having a problem with someone. If you choose not to try to work it out, your friends may become angry.

2. It's important for adults to remember that some kids really don't quite know how to work things out, and need some extra help in learning how. If this happens to you, ask an adult for help.

3. Working things out can be a very difficult thing to do. Most people would prefer to have things their own way all the time, but it's important to remember that just isn't possible.

4. A good method for working things out is to first listen to the other person's point of view, opinion or idea. Then politely tell them your idea and why you might disagree. Then see if you can compromise* on a new idea or solution to the problem.

5. An example of how to work things out would be if you both wanted to be the "red" player in a game, you could say: "You want to be red, but so do I. How about we take turns being red, and flip a coin to see who goes first?"

6. Using a choosing game (see Choosing Game Tips) is always a good way to decide something.

7. Checking on the rules (you can check online if they are not in the game box) is also a fair way to work things out.

8. Sometimes it's a good idea just to decide that friendship is more important than being right, going first, or winning a game. Being willing to occasionally be the person that is willing to be more flexible than the other person is the right choice. But if a friend always wants their own way, it's important for you to stick up for your ideas or wants too.

9. Use the three "C's:" Cooperate,* Collaborate,* and Compromise.*

10. If you get really stuck on something, maybe it's time to agree to disagree and come up with a whole new idea or game to play.

*See glossary for definition.

> *"Thou shouldst not decide until thou hast heard what both have to say."*
>
> -- Aristophanes

www.HowToMakeAndKeepFriends.com

26

Choosing Games

1. There are lots of ways to choose who goes first in a game or resolve a "who gets to have their choice" kind of a problem.

2. Rock, Paper, Scissors.

3. Eeny, Meeny, Miny, Moe.

4. Spuds Up (also known as One Potato, Two Potato).

5. Who has the closest birthday?

6. Pick a number from 1 to 10 and the closest wins.

7. The youngest or oldest can go first.

8. Flip a coin.

9. Roll the dice or spin the spinner and the highest number wins.

10. Draw straws.

*See glossary for descriptions of choosing games.

"Learn the wisdom of compromise, for it is better to bend a little than to break."

-- Jane Wells

27

Good Sportsmanship

1. Play by the rules. However, try to flexible if others are not following the rules "perfectly." Try not to yell at them for "cheating." Ignore small rule changes, and talk calmly to friends about big rule changes.

2. Realize that it's okay to change a rule if everyone agrees to play by the new rule.

3. Be willing to try or learn something new.

4. Be a good winner or loser. Don't brag if you win or complain if you lose. Say "good game" to the other person.

5. Learn to laugh at yourself if you make a mistake and look on the positive side of things.

6. Share in the success of your friend(s).

7. Be willing to change your plan when things go wrong.

8. Every good sport understands that they cannot always have everything their own way.

9. Good sports have more friends and are liked by other people.

10. Show younger children how to be good sports by setting a good example.

"It is your response to winning and losing that makes you a winner or a loser."

-- Harry Sheehy

28

Working in a Group

1. Working in groups can be a very difficult way for some people to work but sometimes there is no choice.

2. When you are working in a group, take some time to listen to and consider everyone's ideas.

3. Sometimes it's helpful to set a timer for each person to share ideas and have a "talking object" that people can pass around so that only the one holding the object talks while others listen.

4. One person should not run the group or boss others. If someone is being bossy in a group, you could let them know that you or others would like a turn to talk and share ideas. Use an "I – Statement" like "I'd like to hear other ideas too," or "I'd like to share my idea."

5. If people in a group are telling you that you sound bossy or are not in charge, then you should stop talking and start listening to others in the group.

6. Figure out the best way for each person to contribute to the project. Maybe someone is great at artwork and someone else is great at making lists of what needs to be done.

7. Share the work that needs to be done fairly.

8. Set something called a deadline for each person, which is a time when each group member promises to have his or her part finished.

9. Sometimes a group member may not do his or her fair share – and even if you try to tell group members to do their part, they just might not. Ask an adult for help or realize that sometimes you may have to work harder than you should have to.

10. The best cooperative words you can use when working in a group are "How about we...?" Everyone can share ideas and other people can decide whether or not that idea works or say, "How about we try this instead?" (See Tips for Working Things Out). Avoid telling group members that they have bad ideas.

"Teamwork is the fuel that allows common people to produce uncommon results."

-- Unknown

29

Playground Success

1. Take turns on the swings, slides and other equipment.

2. Climbing "up" the slide when nobody else is using it is okay, but not when others are trying to come down the slide.

3. Be careful not to ruin the fun by holding onto balls, taking things and running away, etc.

4. If you want to play with someone or a few people, it's always better to join the group than to tease them to get their attention (see Joining A Group Tips).

5. Be aware of where your body is and what it is doing to avoid falling, crashing into people and other accidents.

6. If your body is getting over-excited, take a break on a bench or under a tree for a few minutes.

7. Throwing or flinging sand or rocks is not okay because people can get hurt.

8. If there is a problem with rules in a game and you can't solve them without getting into a fight, ask an adult to help you. (See Tips for Working Things Out.)

9. If you are shy, try looking around for another person who looks shy and invite them to do something with you.

10. Follow all of the rules that are posted at the playground.

"Of course, in our grade school, in those days, there were no organized sports at all. We just went out and ran around the school yard for recess."

-- Alan Shepard

30

Being a Good Playdate Guest

1. Arrive on time so your friend doesn't wonder if you are coming. Call them if you are going to be late.

2. Politely greet your friend and his or her parent. Remove your shoes when you go inside.

3. Decide with your friend what activities you are going to do together. It's nice to do what your friend wants to do first.

4. Treat your friend's home and belongings with respect.

5. Ask before you touch or play with anything.

6. If you feel that you are getting bored or tired, try making suggestions for a different activity or game.

7. It is not okay to play with your friend's brother or sister and not the friend.

8. It's not okay to ask for snacks or open the refrigerator.

9. It's not okay to snoop through drawers, closets or cabinets even if you are curious.

10. When your parent arrives to pick you up, it's important to leave without getting upset. Politely say goodbye and thank your friend for having you over. Let them know you'll have them over for a playdate soon.

"All you need in life is confidence and a phone call."

-- Unknown

31

Being a Good Playdate Host

1. When your friend arrives, smile, say hello, introduce him or her to your parent(s) and family members and make him or her feel welcome.

2. Have some activities or games already planned to play with your friend. Ask them if they want to do those activities or play those games. Maybe create a puppet theatre, play some board games, have a craft project, or bake something together.

3. Put away special things that you do not want to share away before your friend comes over.

4. Ask your parent to keep brothers and sisters busy while you have your playdate or find ways to all play together and include everyone.

5. Offer your friend a snack and a drink.

6. When you are the host, it's polite to do the activities that your friend wants to do first.

7. It's also polite to allow your friend to go first in taking turns or sharing something.

8. If the playdate isn't working or is becoming boring, ask a parent to help you figure out what to do next.

9. Be sure to play with the friend and not ignore your friend or read a book, watch TV, or do other things alone.

10. When your friend is picked up, thank them for coming and walk with them to the door. Don't start a new game when his or her parent is waiting. Let your friend know you'll look forward to the next playdate.

"To be a successful host, when a guest arrives say, 'at last!' and when they leave say, 'so soon!'"

-- Unknown

www.HowToMakeAndKeepFriends.com

32

How to Handle Varying House Rules

1. Understand that your family's rules may be different from other people's rules, and that's okay.

2. Remember that when you're at someone's house, you need to follow their family's rules (even if you don't agree with them).

3. If the other family does activities that your family doesn't allow, respectfully tell them "No thanks," or "My parents don't allow me to do that." If you're not sure, you can ask to call home and find out.

4. When you have friends over, you may need to remind them of the rules of your house. Use a friendly voice so they feel welcome.

5. If your friend tries to tempt you into doing something that your family doesn't allow - hold your ground. A good response to use is "My parents really don't have too many rules so I follow the ones they do have."

6. If friends try to pressure you into breaking rules at either house, hold firm and tell them "No thanks."

7. If you break the rules, it's best to admit it and apologize. This will show your family that you are honest and responsible for your actions.

8. If your house rules seem unfair, respectfully tell your parents that you would like to discuss the rules with them, and see if you can agree on changing the rules.

9. If you break the rules at someone else's house, apologize to your friend and his or her parent.

10. Don't make your friend feel badly that his or her house rules are different than yours. Don't say things like "I can't believe your mom doesn't let you do that!" Each family is different and that's okay.

> *"My rules are different from Dad's (or Mom's). Here, I expect you to do your homework before watching TV."*
>
> -- Jennifer Wolf

33

Playdate Strategies and Etiquette

1. You may feel nervous about asking a new friend for a playdate. It's okay to feel nervous but try to ask them anyway. Remember that the very worst thing that could happen is that they say, "No, thank you." Your response should be, "Okay, maybe another time." The best thing is, they may really want to play with you.

2. If you or your friend are very excited and running around, ask if he or she wants to go outside.

3. If your friend says mean things about your family or other friends, tell them to stop.

4. It is not okay to ditch the person you are having a playdate with for their brother or sister or other kids that are around.

5. If you are tired on a playdate, it is not okay to lie down or take a nap. If you are tired (or don't feel well) you should tell your host (or parent) and you should re-schedule the playdate.

6. If your friend is playing roughly with your things and you're worried he or she might break something, ask them to be more gentle.

7. Try to remember on a playdate that friendship should win over being right about something or beating someone at a game.

8. If you and your friend can't agree on what to do, the best thing to do would to be gracious and do your friend's choice, or the second best thing would be to do a choosing game. (See Choosing Game Tips.)

9. If you run into problems or difficulties on a playdate that you can't solve yourself, ask an adult to help solve it.

10. If you have a feeling that a playdate didn't go well, think about what might have happened and how you might have changed something. It's always helpful to talk to a grown-up about it.

"Friendship isn't a big thing –
it's a million little things."

-- Unknown

www.HowToMakeAndKeepFriends.com

34

Declining a Playdate or

Invitation to Play

1. Declining (saying no to) an invitation to play is okay, but it is important to do so in a way that doesn't hurt the other person's feelings. Say "No thanks, maybe later."

2. If you are invited to do an activity (such as playing a board game with someone) but you are busy or happy doing something else, it is okay to say, "I'd like to play that with you later, but right now I'd like to work on my building project."

3. Or you could also say, "I would like to play with you, can you give me a couple of minutes to finish what I'm doing?"

4. It's not okay to say, "No, I don't want to play with you" or "Go away, I'm busy."

5. If you'd like to play, but the game doesn't interest you, you could say, "I'd like to play with you, but I'm not a big fan of chess, is there something else we could do together instead?"

6. If you are invited for a playdate or to a party and don't know if you can attend, you can say, "Thank

you so much for inviting me, I have to check to see if I can go."

7. If you've been asked to play several times by someone who you want to play with, offer another day that might fit your schedule, so they know that you want to play.

8. If you are invited for a playdate and for some reason you can't go, it's important to call your friend to let them know that you need to reschedule.

9. If a friend asks if they can come to your house without you inviting them first, it's okay to say that it's not a good time or that you need to check your family's schedule first.

10. If you are invited for playdates a lot by someone that you really don't want to play with, it is okay to say that it's just been really busy and your not sure when your schedule will allow you to play, but thank them for the invitation. Eventually they will begin asking other people for playdates.

"Be able to decline a date so gracefully that the person isn't embarrassed that he or she asked."

-- Marilyn vos Savant

www.HowToMakeAndKeepFriends.com

35

Attending Parties

1. If an invitation has an RSVP on it, it means that you need to either accept or decline the invitation – usually by a certain date. It is considered rude not to respond at all, even if you can't make it.

2. Try to find out a little bit about the party. What kind of party is it (for example, birthday)? Ask what you should bring.

3. Try to keep an open mind about the party and what might happen there. Maybe your favorite cake is chocolate, but the person might be having an ice cream cake. Maybe the mom is giving out party bags, but maybe not. It's best not to ask for a party bag.

4. Thank the host when you arrive for inviting you to the party. If you have brought a gift, ask them where you should place it (maybe they will just take it from you and that's okay too).

5. If you are not sure what to do, look around and see what other people are doing and copy that.

6. If you don't know anyone at the party besides the person who invited you, see if there is someone

else who looks like they don't know anyone either and say hello. It's also okay to go to the host and ask them to introduce you to people.

7. Most of the time if there is food placed out on tables (chips, veggies, etc.) it is okay to help yourself to a reasonable amount. Double dipping your food into dips or putting food back once you have touched it is never okay since it can spread germs. If you don't like something, just leave it on your plate or throw it away.

8. Stay in the rooms or area where the party is being held. It is not okay to walk through people's houses or go through their things.

9. If you don't want to participate in the party games, it is okay to watch, but not okay to say that you are bored.

10. Make sure you leave the party with a nice goodbye and thank you.

"Never be the first to arrive at a party or the last to go home and never, never be both."

-- David Brown

www.HowToMakeAndKeepFriends.com

36

Giving and Receiving Gifts

1. When you are choosing a gift for someone, think about what he or she is interested in or what they enjoy.

2. When you give a gift to someone, look him or her in the eye and say something like "I got this for you and I hope you like it."

3. When someone thanks you for a gift, remember to say, "You're welcome."

4. When someone is giving you a gift, wait for him or her to hand it to you and take it gently.

5. Remember to say "thank you" and smile when someone hands you a gift.

6. Open the gift carefully.

7. Grabbing gifts and tearing into paper is considered rude. Helping someone else open a gift is also considered rude unless they've asked.

8. If the gift is something that you already have, just say thank you. If the person asks you if you already have one and would like to exchange it, then it is fine to say that you do.

9. If the gift is something you don't like, this is a situation where it is important that you pretend to like it and say thank you. It is never okay to tell a person that you do not like their gift.

10. Send a thank you note for the gift letting the person know how much you enjoyed their gift.

"The manner of giving is worth more than the gift."

-- Pierre Corneille

37

Social Success in a Restaurant

1. Have your parents help you preview their expectations regarding social behavior and the venue before you go. Expectations at a fast food restaurant are different from those at a fancier restaurant.

2. Bring a bag of quiet activities or play some brain games such as "I Spy" while you are waiting for a table or for your food.

3. Don't stare at others who are eating.

4. Standing on seats, crawling under the table, talking to people you don't know, and running in the restaurant aisles are not acceptable.

5. If you are wiggly and need to stretch, take a short walking break outside or have some "fidget items" to use at the table.

6. Be polite to the person you are ordering from. Look at them when you are ordering and use a strong, clear voice. It's okay to point at what you want on the menu if you can't pronounce it.

7. If you are unsure of what you want to order and you are in a line, step aside and let the next person go.

8. If you don't like what you ordered, you can politely ask to have it changed or fixed.

9. If you finish before everyone else, quietly wait or do more activities.

10. Use good table manners (see Good Table Manners and Meal Etiquette Tips).

"If at first you don't succeed, do it like your mother told you."

-- Unknown

38

Good Table Manners and Meal Etiquette

1. Good manners are important for other people to think well of us.

2. Good manners are important at home, at school, and in public. Practicing manners at home makes it easier to remember them in public.

3. Remember to keep your mouth closed when you are chewing and not talk when your mouth is full of food. Taking small bites makes this easier.

4. Playing with your food is not okay. If you don't like it or don't wish to eat it, just leave it on your plate. Spitting out food or saying "yuck" in a loud voice is also not okay.

5. It is important to wait for everyone to be served before eating and ask to have things passed to you to avoid reaching and grabbing.

6. If you don't like something that is being served, just say, "No, thank you." It is polite to try a little bit of everything that is served.

7. Dinner conversation should be friendly. You could try asking questions such as, "What was the best part of everyone's day today?"

www.HowToMakeAndKeepFriends.com

8. If you spill something by accident, it is your responsibility to help clean it up.

9. When at someone else's home, it's polite to tell the person who cooked that you enjoyed the meal.

10. Put your napkin in your lap and use it as needed.

"Manners are a sensitive awareness of the feelings of others. If you have that awareness, you have good manners, no matter what fork you use."

-- Emily Post

Section #4:

Tips for Handling Social Challenges

39

Managing Mean or "Dirty" Looks

1. Smile – that may stop the mean look right away.

2. Think about what your own facial expression is showing at that moment.

3. Did something just happen that might have made the person mad?

4. Does this person often look like this even when they're not mad?

5. Engage them in light conversation or make a joke to lighten the mood.

6. Ask them if they are okay.

7. Do you think they might be worried about something?

8. Has this person been unkind to you in the past?

9. Look away and find a friendlier person to hang out with.

10. Could something you're wearing or doing cause someone to have an odd or weird thought about you?

"When you change the way you look at things, the things you look at change."

-- Wayne Dyer

40

Handling Lies, Rumors and Secrets

1. Everyone experiences hearing lies, rumors and secrets and it can be very upsetting.

2. It's important that if your friend tells you a secret that you don't tell others.

3. The only time that you would tell your friend's secret is that if someone is going to do something dangerous or there is abuse or bullying happening. If a friend tells you that she thinks a boy is cute, it's not okay to tell.

4. Breaking a confidence that was told to you will likely cause you to lose that friend.

5. If someone wants to tell you a secret that someone else has told him or her, you can say something like, "Please don't tell me anything that you don't want repeated" or "Would Julie be okay with you telling me this?"

6. Rumors and gossip are the same. Usually they are things that people are saying about other people to be hurtful or are embarrassing to someone.

7. Lying is almost always a bad choice in any situation. It will usually go much better for you if

you tell the truth. "Yes, I broke the window and I'll figure out a way to pay to repair it."

8. If you are caught in a lie, it's best to take responsibility and say, "It was wrong of me to lie...what can I do to make it better?"

9. There is something called a "white lie" that is socially acceptable when used to preserve another person's feelings and can't really hurt anyone. This is something like saying "I really like your new haircut" to your friend when you might not really like it.

10. If other friends are gossiping or spreading rumors about someone, tell them that it's not cool, try to change the subject onto something else or find a way to leave the group and not participate in the gossip.

"Say what you mean, mean what you say, but don't say it mean."

-- Unknown

41

How to Handle Rejection, "Clubs," and Being Treated Unfairly

1. It's important to remember that while we would very much like everyone to like us all the time that unfortunately we are going to meet people that are not nice or who treat us unfairly.

2. If other children are being mean or unfair, it's important to remember that if you let them upset you, they will only do it more.

3. If other kids are excluding you or not allowing you to be in their club or not inviting you to their parties, don't let them see you upset. You can say something like, "Wow, I don't understand why you want to be so mean" and just walk away.

4. Instead of becoming upset or "begging" other kids to let you play, come to their party, or be in their club, walk away and look for other friends.

5. Try not to ask questions that will get you rejected or excluded. Say, "Hey guys, show me what the club is doing" rather than asking, "Can I join the club?" Try not to ask questions that can be answered with a no.

6. Usually a "club" has a leader. Maybe there are some other kids in the club that will see that the leader is being mean and may want to leave the club and play with you.

7. If you feel that you were treated unfairly, such as being called "out" in a game, consider that it might have been an honest mistake the first time it happens. If you keep getting called "out" over and over when you are not, then it is time to handle it as something being done on purpose. You could say "I feel like I'm being called 'out' when I'm not. How about we review the rules again?"

8. It's also very important (and a very hard thing to do) to ask yourself what it is that you might be doing or saying that might cause other children to leave you out or not invite you. Do you do some things that might seem annoying to other people? Do you sound bossy sometimes?

9. You can find a grown-up and let them know that you are having a difficult time trying to find someone to play with and maybe they could help you get a game going with some other kids.

10. Just remember that if certain kids or friends don't work out, there are lots and lots of other people to be friendly with and that they don't even have to be your own age or at your own school.

42

If Someone is Bullying, Teasing or Hurting You

1. Tell them to stop (this takes courage but it's important).

2. Get away from them.

3. Tell an adult that you told the person to stop and that you got away from them, so they know that you have already done the first two steps.

4. Try not to be a victim of bullying by following the tips in the Weird Thoughts section.

5. Avoid kids who tend to be mean to other kids.

6. When making new friends, watch for comments from them that sound like bullying (for example: "I hate that kid, he's such a nerd.")

7. Try to be around other kids so you aren't alone.

8. Try to make some nice friends that you can feel safe with.

9. Don't blame yourself; it's not your fault.

10. Bullying is serious, so tell an adult and visit http://www.stopbullyingnow.hrsa.gov/kids/ for more information.

"Promise me you'll always remember: You're braver than you believe, and stronger than you seem, and smarter than you think."

-- Christopher Robin to Pooh

43

If Someone is Bullying or Teasing Others

1. If you feel safe, tell them to "knock it off" or say, "That's not cool."

2. Ask the victim if they are okay.

3. Keep an eye out for the victim during lunch, recess, or at the bus to see if they are getting bullied.

4. Discuss the situation with an adult, and remember that telling about bullying is not tattling.

5. Encourage the victim to discuss the situation with an adult and remind them that telling an adult is not tattling.

6. Consider your own friendship with the bully – should you continue to befriend them or maybe decide to find some new friends.

7. Don't spread rumors about someone else even if you know them to be true.

8. Don't forward e-mails or online messages that say negative things about someone else.

9. Avoid "clubs" or groups that consistently exclude other kids.

www.HowToMakeAndKeepFriends.com

10. Bullying is very serious, so tell an adult and visit **http://www.stopbullyingnow.hrsa.gov/kids/do-you-witness-bullying.aspx** for more information.

"Sometimes the biggest act of courage is a small one."

-- Lauren Raffo

44

If You are Bullying Someone

1. Think about how it would feel if the same were being done to you and stop.

2. Talk to an adult about the feelings you are getting out of bullying someone.

3. If someone is hurting you, tell a trusted adult immediately.

4. Bullying others is very serious – find out more about how to stop at **http://www.stopbullyingnow.hrsa.gov/kids/do-you-bully.aspx**.

5. There are laws against bullying and if you continue to bully, you could get into legal trouble.

6. Try being nice to the person you are bullying and get to know them better.

7. Do you want to have people think of you as a bully? Reputations can be hard to shake, so bullying should stop right way.

8. If you want to stop bullying but are having a hard time stopping, ask your friends to help you stop.

9. If you're angry or frustrated, find ways to resolve conflicts and manage your anger without taking it out on others.

10. Be courageous and take responsibility for your actions.

"The antidote for 50 enemies is one friend."

-- Aristotle

45

Balance of Power in Friendships

1. Understand that each friendship should have a balance of power that is comfortable for both friends.

2. When someone always gets his or her way and the other always gives in, then there is an imbalance of power.

3. An imbalance of power also happens when one friend always calls the other to get together, but the other friend doesn't call back or never invites him or her to do things together.

4. To regain that balance, encourage fairness without anger. For example, "How about if I go first this time since you went first last time?"

5. If your friend always says that your ideas are bad, tell your friend that if he or she is not going to ever do things your way, then you're not interested in playing. It's important to say this in a normal, not an angry, voice. Just state it very matter-of-factly.

6. Choices give you power. You have the choice to stop playing if kids are being unfair and you have the choice to walk away from uncomfortable situations.

7. Remember to not impose your power over someone else.

8. Always think about how you would feel if you were in their situation.

9. Over time, if it seems like your friend is always "one-upping" you (for example: they are always bigger, better, stronger, smarter, etc.), then decide if that is a friend that you should spend time with.

10. You are as important as anyone else and no one has the power to make you feel as though you are less important than they are.

"Don't walk in front of me, I may not follow. Don't walk behind me, I may not lead. Walk beside me and be my friend."

-- Albert Camus

46

Peer Pressure to Do "Bad" Things

1. Sometimes other kids may try to get you to do bad things or things you know that you are not supposed to do. This is called peer pressure.

2. Even though you may want to be someone's friend very badly, if they are pressuring you to do something you are not comfortable doing or that you know is wrong, they are not being a real friend.

3. If someone is doing something wrong (like swearing) and wants you to do it too, you have the choice to say no. Remember choice is power.

4. You can make a joke and then change the subject.

5. You can offer a reason why you don't want to, like "if my soccer coach heard me swearing, I'd be thrown off the team."

6. "Use" your parents...say "if my parents heard me say that, I'd be grounded forever."

7. Just firmly say that you don't want to or that it's "lame" and you're not doing it.

8. Walk away from the uncomfortable situation.

www.HowToMakeAndKeepFriends.com

9. You can pretend you didn't hear it and just ignore it.

10. Have other friends "back you up," and hold your ground despite the pressure.

"Never do a wrong thing to make a friend or to keep one."

-- Robert E. Lee

47

How to Get Help From an Adult

1. Sometimes problems are difficult to solve all by yourself.

2. If you don't know how to work it out, it's okay to ask for help.

3. Remember that it's better to ask for help than get caught in a fight or do something that will get you in trouble.

4. You should first try to solve the problem yourself by trying a choosing game, reading the rules, saying, "How about we try…" or another problem solving strategy. First, say "No" to the person who you are having a problem with. You can say, "I don't like what you are doing (or saying) and I want you to stop please." If they don't stop, you can say it again with a little more "muscle" in your voice.

5. If that doesn't work, then you "go." That means try to take yourself away from the problem by walking away.

6. Sometimes that doesn't work either, and the person will continue to do what they are doing. In that case, it's time to "tell," or ask an adult for help.

7. You want to make sure that you ask an adult for help the correct way and not by tattling. Tell the adult that you have tried both "no and go" and you need some help.

8. Approach the adult by getting their attention and then saying "I need to talk to you about something."

9. When discussing your problem with an adult, try to stay calm.

10. Share the main points and fill in details as necessary.

"There are times when two people need to step apart from one another, but there is no rule that says they have to turn and fire."

-- Robert Breault

www.HowToMakeAndKeepFriends.com

48

Knowing Who is a Good Friend

1. A good friend genuinely likes you and wants to spend time you. A good friend usually has a lot of the same interests as you.

2. A good friend does not just want to spend time with you just to use your video games, swim in your pool, etc.

3. A good friend does not insult you, put you down, or try to make you do things that will get you in trouble.

4. A good friend will ask you if you are okay and if they can help when you feel sad.

5. A good friend accepts you for who you are and doesn't try to change you or make you act differently.

6. If you sometimes or often don't feel good being around a certain friend, he/she is likely not a good friend.

7. A good friend sticks up for you and always "has your back." A good friend cheers your successes and doesn't make you feel "less than" anyone.

8. A good friend is always your friend, even when other kids who aren't your friends are around or if you are friends with another person that some people don't like.

9. A good friend does not have to be the same age, the same grade or in your school – they can be anyone.

10. And of course, if you want to be that good friend in return, you should do all these same things!

"You need to have that one friend that is always there for you. It makes you feel safe and wanted inside."

-- Trent B.

49

Handling Jealousy When Your Friend Makes a New Friend

1. Jealous feelings are when you wish you had something that someone else has (friend, toy, or an experience). Everyone has jealous feelings sometimes so it's important to know that you're not alone.

2. Remember that people can have a lot of different friends and that it doesn't mean they like you any less.

3. Sometimes when people make a new friend, it's really exciting for a while and they may want to spend a lot of time getting to know that other person. It doesn't mean that they think any less of your friendship.

4. Perhaps you could try to get to know the other person too and maybe all of you could hang out as a group.

5. Your friend may not know that their other friendship is causing you to have jealous feelings so try not to be angry with them.

6. Give your friend a little space and spend time with your other friends for a little while.

www.HowToMakeAndKeepFriends.com

7. Invite your friend over to hang out and spend some time solidifying your friendship.

8. Ask yourself if you have done anything to make your friend angry or jealous at some point and if they are spending time with new friends because they feel jealous or angry.

9. Remember that each friend you have (and that other people have) fulfills a different friendship need. You may have friends who you like to talk to, others who you can feel safe playing rough with, and others who are great to play video games with. Your friend could be spending time with the other friend because they are filling a different friendship need.

10. Next time you're with your friend, ask something about their life to show that you care about them.

> " 'Pooh,' he whispered. 'Yes, Piglet?' 'Nothing,' said Piglet, taking Pooh's paw. 'I just wanted to be sure of you.' "
>
> -- A. A. Milne

50

When Friendships Change

1. Friendships may change as you grow older, as the things you like to do may change.

2. If a friendship ends, it may be because of these changes, and not anyone's "fault."

3. If a friend stops calling you to hang out or is spending time with other friends instead, think about whether you still like the same things.

4. Think about if you had an argument, or if he/she has been frustrated while playing lately.

5. Do you feel like when they were with you that they really wanted to be there or did they seem distracted?

6. Give the friend some space by not contacting them for a while. They may just need a break from the friendship and may want to hang out again someday.

7. Talk to a trusted adult or friend about how you're feeling about the friendship changing. Chances are they have been through this before and will understand, and may have some ideas.

8. When you think about the friendship, consider if it was a good fit for you. Some friendships hang on because of convenience or parental friendships, and not because the friendship was a quality one. You deserve to have really good friends who care about you. You may find that you're happier with the new friends you make.

9. Spend time with your other friends and develop those friendships instead of trying to revive a friendship that may not be working for you right now.

10. It may take time to find a new close friend, but it **will happen,** so remind yourself to hang in there.

"Some people come into our lives and quickly go. Some stay for a while, leave footprints on our hearts, and we are never, ever the same."

-- Flavia Weedn

A Note to Kids

We are so happy that you read our book, and we hope that you found new ideas in these tips that will help you make and keep good friends!

Miss Nadine and Miss Donna have helped many children learn how to make friends by running after school friendship clubs for kids at the Peter Pan Center, which Miss Donna opened in Massachusetts in 2002: **www.peterpancenter.com**.

Miss Nadine has a friendship website that your parents can visit at **www.socialsmartkids.com**.

We know that everyone can learn how to make friends with practice. You can share this book with your parents, a social coach or your guidance counselor at school and ask them to help you with some of the ideas. The more you practice, the easier it will become!

You can pick just one tip at a time to practice so that it doesn't feel too hard - for example, just work on the "Personal Space" tips first, and then move on to the next set of tips when that one becomes easier.

You, your parents, or a counselor might even have more tips and ideas! We'd love to hear about them! We'd also

www.HowToMakeAndKeepFriends.com

love to know what parts of our book you found the most helpful. Send us an e-mail (with your parents' permission) about how our tips helped you make a friend!

Happy Friendship Making!

Miss Donna & Miss Nadine

Miss Donna's e-mail is dshea@peterpancenter.com

Miss Nadine's e-mail is nbriggs@socialsmartkids.com

www.HowToMakeAndKeepFriends.com

A Note to Parents:
Next Steps

Thank you for choosing our book for your child. It is our sincere hope that you and your child found new and renewed ideas to assist in not only rudimentary social skills for home, at school and the community, but those will carry your child into deep and lasting friendships.

This guide is based on tips that we have found helpful in our work with children who have mild to moderate social challenges. Guidance counselors and educators may also find this book helpful in starting discussions with children who participate in "lunch bunches" or other social opportunities at school. Families that have children with more significant social and communication needs may find that this book is a useful "jumping off" place or a great reference guide as they access other, more in-depth social curriculum.

In providing this book for your child, you have taken a great step in assisting your child to build and maintain friendships. We can't stress enough how vitally important parent and adult coaching is to the success of children in building this skills. Hosting playdates and providing social opportunities allow children to practice these crucial skills in "real time." For fun and easy ways parents can provide these opportunities, feel free to download ideas on our website, www.HowToMakeAndKeepFriends.com.

For parents and adults who are working with children experiencing social challenges, it is important to "partner" with the child to be successful, rather than take a more authoritarian approach to behaviors that need changing. The two most important social skills that a child will ever learn are **empathy and respect**. As adult partners "lead" by example...children are sure to follow.

Nadine Briggs & Donna Shea

Suggested Reading

For Parents

The Explosive Child: A New Approach For Understanding And Parenting Easily Frustrated, Chronically Inflexible Children (Author: Ross W. Greene)

Lost at School: Why Our Kids With Behavioral Challenges Are Falling Through The Cracks And How We Can Help Them (Author: Ross W. Greene)

It's So Much Work To Be Your Friend: Helping the Child With Learning Disabilities Find Social Success (Author: Richard Lavoie)

The Out-of-Sync Child: Recognizing And Coping With Sensory Processing Disorder (Author: Carol Kranowitz)

The Out-of-Sync Child Has Fun, Revised Edition: Activities for Kids With Sensory Processing Disorder (Author: Carol Kranowitz)

The Unwritten Rules of Friendship: Simple Strategies to Help Your Child Make Friends (Authors: Natalie Madorsky Elman and Eileen Kennedy-Moore)

www.HowToMakeAndKeepFriends.com

Suggested Reading

For Kids

Stick Up For Yourself: Every Kid's Guide To Personal Power & Positive Self-Esteem (Authors: Gershen Kaufman, Lev Raphael and Pamela Espeland)

A Volcano In My Tummy: Helping Children To Handle Anger (Authors: Eliane Whitehouse and Warwick Pudney)

How To Take The Grrrr Out Of Anger (Laugh and Learn) (Authors: Elizabeth Verdick and Marjorie Lisovskis)

What To Do When You Worry Too Much: A Kid's Guide To Overcoming Anxiety (What To Do Guides for Kids) (Author: Dawn Huebner, PhD)

What To Do When Your Temper Flares: A Kid's Guide To Overcoming Problems With Anger (What to Do Guides for Kids) (Author: Dawn Huebner, PhD)

What To Do When Your Brain Gets Stuck: A Kid's Guide To Overcoming OCD (What-To-Do Guides For Kids) (Author: Dawn Huebner, PhD)

www.HowToMakeAndKeepFriends.com

What to Do When You Grumble Too Much: A Kid's Guide To Overcoming Negativity (What To Do Guides For Kids) (Author: Dawn Huebner, PhD)

*Sensitive Sam: Sam's Sensory Adventure Has A Happy Ending! (*Author: Marla Roth-Fisch)

Glossary of Friendship Terms and Choosing Games

Assuming – to take something for granted or form an opinion without proof.

Bullying – the act of intimidating or scaring another person to make them do something.

Collaborate – to work together.

Compromise – settling a disagreement so that both people get a little of what they want.

Cooperate – the same as collaborate.

Embarrassment – feeling ashamed or uncomfortable about something done or said in public.

Etiquette – the rules of socially acceptable behavior.

Expectations – what someone wants you to do in a situation.

Expression – a showing of feeling on the face.

Flexible – adjustable to change.

Gracious – courteous or polite.

Hoarding – keeping everything for oneself.

Impulsivity – acting without thinking first.

Inferring – coming to conclusions based on what you think or see about something.

Jealousy – being resentful or envious about something someone else has or does.

Modulate – to regulate, adjust and adapt.

Non-Verbal Communication – signals sent by faces and bodies about what people are thinking or feeling.

Observe – to notice or pay attention to.

Opinion – a belief in one's own mind about something.

Peer Pressure – pressure from friends to behave in the same way or to do something wrong.

Perception – awareness of an idea or situation on which you form an opinion.

Reaction – a response to something that has happened.

Rumors – general talk or an unconfirmed story not based on actual truth.

Solution – a method of solving a problem.

Strategy – a plan for achieving a goal.

Rock, Paper, Scissors

The players count aloud to three, or speak the name of the game (e.g. "Rock! Paper! Scissors!"), each time raising one hand in a fist and swinging it down on the count. On the third count (saying, "Scissors!"), the players change their hands into one of three gestures, which they then "throw" by extending it towards their opponent. Variations include a version where players use a fourth count — "Shoot!" — before throwing their gesture, or a version where they only shake their hands twice before "throwing." Others prefer a five count cadence by saying "Says Shoot!" before throwing their gesture. The gestures are:

- **Rock**, represented by a clenched fist.
- **Scissors**, represented by the index and middle fingers extended and separated
- **Paper**, represented by an open hand, with the fingers connected (horizontal).

The objective is to select a gesture which defeats that of the opponent. Gestures are resolved as follows:

- Rock blunts or breaks scissors: that is, rock defeats scissors
- Scissors cut paper: scissors defeats paper
- Paper covers, sands or captures rock: paper defeats rock

If both players choose the same gesture, the game is tied and the players throw again.

Source: http://en.wikipedia.org/wiki/Rock-paper-scissors

Flip a Coin

During coin flipping, the coin is tossed into the air such that it rotates end-over-end several times. Either beforehand or when the coin is in the air, an interested party calls "heads" or "tails", indicating which side of the coin that party is choosing. The other party is assigned the opposite side. Depending on custom, the coin may be caught, caught and inverted, or allowed to land on the ground. When the coin comes to rest, the toss is complete and the party who called or was assigned the face-up side is declared the winner. If the outcome is unclear the toss is repeated.

Source: http://en.wikipedia.org/wiki/Coin_flipping

Drawing straws

Drawing straws is a selection method used by a group to choose one person to do a task when no one has volunteered for it. The same practice could also be used to choose one of several volunteers should an agreement not be reached.

The group leader takes a number of straws or similar long cylindrical objects, and makes sure one of them is physically shorter than the rest. He then grabs all the straws in his fist such that all of them appear to be of the same length.

The leader then offers the clenched fist to the group. Each member of the group draws a straw from the fist. At the end of the offering, the person with the shortest straw is the one who must do the task.

Source: http://en.wikipedia.org/wiki/Drawing_straws

www.HowToMakeAndKeepFriends.com

Eeny, meeny, miny, moe

"Eeny, meeny, miny, moe", which can be spelled a number of ways, is a children's counting rhyme, used to select a person to be "it". It is one of a large group of similar 'Counting-out rhymes' where the child pointed-to by the chanter on the last syllable is 'counted out'.

Source:
http://en.wikipedia.org/wiki/Eeny,_meeny,_miny,_moe

Spuds up

Each person puts their fists forward (their 'spuds' meaning potatoes). One person chants "One potato, two potato, three potato four, five potato, six potato, seven potato, more." with each word pointing to the next spud going round clockwise. The 'spud' on which the word "more" falls is eliminated and the player holds that hand behind their back. The chant starts again from the next spud. When a player has both their spuds eliminated they are out until there is only one winner.

Source: http://en.wikipedia.org/wiki/Selection_methods

About the Authors

Donna Shea, Director of the Peter Pan Center, and Nadine Briggs, Founder of Social Smart Kids, are passionate about helping kids make and keep friends. They have dedicated themselves to working with children who experience mild to moderate social difficulties, and understand that social nuances can and should be taught.

Donna and Nadine have teamed up to form the **Social Success in School** initiative. This comprehensive group of programs for students, educators and parents are designed to foster positive social skills and interactions among students to prevent bullying. Popular workshops include "Getting the Mads Out," "Behavior Begins with Respect," "Good Sports Always Win," and "Ending the Cycle of Bullying." To learn more, visit

www.SocialSuccessInSchool.com

www.HowToMakeAndKeepFriends.com

About Donna Shea and The Peter Pan Center

In order to be a friend, you need to have a friend. At the Peter Pan Center, helping kids make and keep lasting friendships is our passion. The mission of the Peter Pan Center is to create a safe and welcoming atmosphere to give children ages 4-15 the opportunity to learn and practice friendship skills.

Whatever the barrier to friendship a child faces ~ be it behavioral issues, social anxiety and conversational skills, inability to read social cues, anger management challenges, etc. ~ we have used our in-the-moment coaching model to effectively support children in overcoming these hurdles since the Center opened in 2002.

Kids are not our only passion - parents are too! Here at the Peter Pan Center, we help parents learn to manage difficult behaviors, coach their child toward social success, work with school systems and more!

The Center's Director, Donna Shea, is a behaviorist and parent educator holding a B.A. in Behavioral Science from Lesley University in Cambridge, MA. She works in

www.HowToMakeAndKeepFriends.com

collaboration with numerous resources and professionals to address the needs of families struggling with learning, behavioral, and social challenges.

Donna also acts as a behavioral consultant to pre-schools, schools, parent groups, and human service agencies. She provides foster parent training for the New England Foster Care Association. She also travels to bring professional development and parent workshops to groups and venues outside the local area. She has a certification in training others in Bullying and Cyberbullying Prevention through the Massachusetts Aggression Reduction Center (MARC). Donna brings 24 years of life experience to her work as a parent of two sons with ADHD.

Donna works as a consultant to families focusing on teaching and supporting effective parenting techniques as well as offering programs geared toward children's social and behavioral success, including one of the only anger management programs for children in the local area. The approach is directive and solution-based, utilizing collaborative problem solving, creative ideas, suggestions, strategies, and referrals to other resources as needed.

www.PeterPanCenter.com

THE PETER PAN CENTER
Where Friends Are Made

www.HowToMakeAndKeepFriends.com

About Nadine Briggs and Social Smart Kids

Social Smart Kids is dedicated to educating and supporting kids with social challenges. Since 2006, Social Smart Kids has provided online support, and a wide variety of social skills products and services to children, their parents, and school systems to coach children who have difficulty forming meaningful friendships. Social Smart Kids believes that, although all children struggle socially at some point during their childhood, those who experience more frequent and consistent social awkwardness need adults to intervene and explicitly teach them social skills. Some children, particularly those with certain types of special needs, have a very difficult time making friends, developing solid friendships, and keeping friends. Social Smart Kids believes that every child is capable of improving their social skills with the appropriate support offered in the home, school, and community environments.

The founder of Social Smart Kids, Nadine Briggs, focused primarily on social skills with her daughter who was born in 1996 with Down syndrome. She believes that teaching her daughter to be socially appropriate has been the life lesson that will lead to her future successes. Through years of experience integrating her daughter into society, she shares a parent-involvement philosophy which has worked well for her and for other parents she has counseled. Nadine also has a son and has recognized the need for teaching social skills to children of all abilities, and not only to children with special needs.

Nadine is a parent consultant trained through the Federation for Children with Special Needs, a member of the Massachusetts Down Syndrome Congress Educational Task Force, the Parent Coordinator for the Massachusetts Down Syndrome Congress, a social coach and a certified Sibshop facilitator. She has a certification in training others in Bullying and Cyberbullying Prevention through the Massachusetts Aggression Reduction Center (MARC). Nadine is co-creator with Donna Shea of the Social Success in School anti-bullying initiative, which is designed to improve social competency and reduce bullying.

Social Smart Kids offers a multitude of services including: social skills coaching for parents and kids, IEP consults for social skills goals and support, the Social Smart Kidskits program, Social Smart Kids Discussion Cards, the Social Smart KidsCamp summer program, Classroom Chats to explain special needs to classmates, workshops, seminars, sibling support, and valuable information regarding social barriers on www.SocialSmartKids.com.

www.HowToMakeAndKeepFriends.com